A Green City Program
For San Francisco Bay Area Cities And
Towns

Arising From
Symposia on Urban Sustainability In
The San Francisco Bay Area
Held at Fort Mason Center, San Francisco
Spring and Summer, 1986

A Green City Program
For San Francisco Bay Area Cities And
Towns

written and edited by
Peter Berg
Beryl Magilavy
Seth Zuckerman

Planet Drum Books
San Francisco, California
1989

Cover art by Anthony Holdsworth
Cover design by Peter Kunz
Illustrations by Val Mina

Publication of the Green City Program was made possible by the generous support of:

Earth First! Foundation
The Haight Ashbury Neighborhood Council
Rex Foundation
The L. J. Skaggs and Mary C. Skaggs Foundation
and
The Members and Supporters of
Planet Drum Foundation

© 1989 by Planet Drum Books, San Francisco
Printed in the United States of America

ISBN: 0-937102-02-4.

This book is a collaborative effort of many Bay Area groups and individuals. Special thanks to some of the many who contributed time and effort:

Delaine Anderson, lists coordination
Marie Dolcini, production
Stephanie Fulton, secretarial work
Judy Goldhaft, meeting coordination
Mary Gomes, benefit coordination
Marc Kasky, meeting facilitation
Robert MacKimmie, layout
Bonnie Monte, editing
Michael Phillips, small business expertise
Susan Swift, publicity
Holbrook Teter, book design
Stephanie Troyon, publicity
Marylou Vanderventer, recycling expertise
and
Karen Wilhelm-Buckley, publication format

CONTENTS

Introduction

"Well, I went down to the creek and found a willow tree with low branches and climbed up into it."

A circle of bioregional workshop participants sat at the base of wave-patterned red rocks in San Francisco's Glen Canyon Park. White chalk handprints resembling Stone Age pictographs mark the rock faces, left behind by climbers who practice there. Each person in the group had been asked to go on a "vision quest" within the fifty-foot-wide swath of native vegetation bordering a small creek that drains part of Twin Peaks and flows through the park. Despite the fact that several-storied buildings ring a good part of the canyon rim close by, the creek area is still a wild place that probably hasn't changed much over the last 10,000 years. Several species of small mammals still make their homes there.

"I sat in the tree in a way that I couldn't see anybody else, just the other willows along the creek."

The quest had simple guidelines: be alone and don't talk to or even see anyone else for at least a half-hour; think about how you are connected to the native plants and animals, watersheds, land forms, climate, and other natural features of the Northern California bioregion. A conch shell had been blown to summon everyone back.

The speaker worked as a legal secretary in the city. Now it was her turn to tell what natural insight or experience she had just discovered. "I was there for maybe ten minutes when a very large bird landed on a branch just a few feet directly above me. It preened its wings and orange–red tail feathers right in front of the sun. Then it settled in and stayed awhile before eventually flying away.

It was really big so I think it must have been a red-tailed hawk."

Everyone stared at her with the mixture of incredulity and envy that should deservedly fall on someone who comes in such close contact with this avian superstar. Red-tailed hawks are high-strung hunters who rarely fail to see other animals near them, usually long before they themselves are seen. The persistence of predator birds in the city is a minor miracle in itself. That one of them revealed itself so intimately to one of the vision questers seemed much too unlikely and purposeful to be simple coincidence. Could it be an act of recognition for the group's effort to find and respect wildness in the midst of urban pavement and exhaust fumes?

Any threat of solemnity evaporated in laughter when she asked with innocent hopefulness whether there would be another workshop like this one soon. What would have to happen to satisfy her expectations next time? Coyotes singing in Golden Gate Park?

* * *

The San Francisco Bay Area is unique in so many ways that its most common characteristic is probably diversity. Differences in natural characteristics range from Pacific tide pools to redwood forests, from flat, bird-filled marshes to the abrupt rise of Mt. Diablo from where the Sierra Nevada Mountains can be seen more than a hundred miles across the Central Valley. A diversity of people matches that of the bioregion. Inhabitants generally pride themselves on being tolerant, but the truth is that if they weren't, they would probably be miserable. Italian Catholics go to school with Chinese Buddhists, surviving hippies rent apartments in the same buildings as prosperous yuppies, Latinos speak Spanish to Filipinos, and recently arrived Southeast Asians who don't speak each other's languages raise children together and build strong communities in formerly destitute downtown areas. Thousands of immigrants from foreign countries and just as many from the rest of the United States stream in constantly to find opportunities for both work and self-expression. Who can blame them? The Bay Area is one of the most naturally-endowed and enlightened life-places on the planet.

There are growing cracks in the surface of this benign picture however, and they can eventually grow to be more devastating than anything that could emanate from the San Andreas fault. Here's the problem: *No large urban area in North America is sustainable at present. How can the Bay Area expect to absorb the additional two-thirds of a million people that is predicted by the beginning of the twenty-first century without losing its livability?*

Cities aren't sustainable because they have become dependent on distant, rapidly shrinking sources for the basic essentials of food, water, energy and materials. At the same time they have severely damaged the health of local systems upon which any sensible notion of sustainability must ultimately depend. Watercourses have become dumps for everything from petrochemicals to sewage, nearby farmland is continually lost to housing developments, soil and watertables are poisoned by seepage wastes from garbage buried in landfills, fossil fuel emissions increasingly mar the purity of air, and the small refuges for wildlife and native vegetation that still remain are constantly reduced or threatened.

These problems are worsening at a faster rate in the San Francisco Bay Area than in many other urban centers. In addition, the social benefits that make cities livable, such as a sense of community and wide civic participation, are more typically eroded rather than strengthened as the megalopolis that surrounds the Bay continues to grow.

The situation is critical, yet there hasn't been a comprehensive movement to create a saving alternative. There isn't a single realistic plan in operation to ecologically redirect and thereby advance the quality of life for any sizable urban area in North America.

What would it take to establish a positive outcome for the seemingly overwhelming problems of cities? What features of city life should be addressed and in what ways? How would an alternative approach for the future look and feel?

* * *

First it's necessary to understand that the nature of cities has already changed tremendously in just the last few decades. In 1950 about two-thirds of North Americans lived in cities or towns of 25,000 or more, but by 1986 the proportion had jumped to 75% of an overall population that had itself increased significantly. To accommodate this tidal wave of new residents, the sheer number and size of cities has grown very rapidly. Mexico City is the most dramatic example, almost doubling its population from 8 to 14 million between 1970 and 1980. Since then it has swollen to over 20 million to become the most populous city that has ever existed. The movement of people from the countryside into cities is one of this century's strongest demographic trends, one that promises to continue into the future. Urban-dwelling, once the rarest way for people to live, is fast becoming the dominant form of human inhabitation on the planet.

The San Francisco Bay Area's population grew from 4.6 to 5.2 million between 1970 and 1980, and is around 5.8 million at present. About 6.5 million people are expected to live in the region by the year 2000. That means that the rate of population increase in only 30 years will have been more than an astonishing 40%.

But while the size and number of cites is growing so drastically, there hasn't been an appropriately directed change in the way people live in them. City-dwelling is still imagined as a special and privileged condition that is supported by a surrounding hinterland with rural workers to provide necessities. The fact that city living is now the norm for the vast majority of North Americans hasn't really penetrated popular awareness. The vast scale of ecological damage that is directly attributable to the ways cities presently function (for instance, roughly 40% of the non-agricultural pollution of San Francisco Bay is simply the result of run-off from city streets) still isn't fully recognized. The demands for resources that cities make on their own bioregions as well as on faraway locations are becoming hundreds of times greater while means to supply them are drying up, but this urgently important issue still hasn't had an impact on the core of municipal policy-making.

There needs to be a profound shift in the fundamental premises and activities of city living. Urban people have to adopt conserver values and carry out more responsible practices in wide areas of daily life. Municipal governments need to restructure their priorities so that long-term sustainability can become a feasible goal. With such a large portion of the population removed from the land and from access to resources, ways to secure some share of the basic requirements of food, water, energy and materials will have to be found within the confines of cities.

Cities need to become "green." They must be transformed into places that are life-enhancing and regenerative.

* * *

There are dozens of sustainability-oriented groups in the Bay Area who, taken together, represent a sizable reservoir of good ideas and willing hands. Planet Drum Foundation has brought together representatives of these groups to develop proposals for an over-arching program of changes that could be supported by the general public in order to prevent further deterioration of the region and lead in the direction of greater self-reliance.

A series of "Green City" meetings, held at San Francisco's Fort Mason Center in 1986, brought together groups and individuals from specific fields of interest who were asked to contribute suggestions and visions. Over 150 representatives attended in person and an equal number added recommendations to written reports of the sessions. The range of participants was usually much broader than any one of them would have predicted, and for most it was a first opportunity to meet their fellow "greeners." At the Recycling and Re-use meeting, for instance, there were not only representatives of some city and county recycling agencies but also a well-rounded showing from private re-use businesses, citizen groups opposed to waste, youth employment agencies, and professional scavenger companies. The Urban Wild Habitat meeting was one of the largest and included nature society members, urban gardeners, defenders of open space, native plant experts, animal-tenders, teachers, environmental writers, the founder of the citizens' group that helped secure the Golden Gate National Recreation Area and even the director of Golden Gate Park. Other meetings were held on the subjects of transportation, urban planting, renewable energy, neighborhood character and empowerment, small businesses and cooperatives, sustainable planning, and celebrating life-place vitality.

Each session began with a description of the current situation from each participant's point of view. Not surprisingly, these accounts portrayed more dismal overall conditions than are usually acknowledged in political rhetoric. Renewable energy advocates complained of no significant gains in using alternatives to fossil fuels since oil resumed a low price in the late 1970s. Neighborhood representatives related how high-rises and chain stores are crowding out the last remnants of unique small businesses and block-scaled social and family life. Community gardeners spoke of losing land to developers because city governments lacked the will to protect it or ensure the acquisition of substitute space. Sustainable planning proponents detailed the failure of residents' influence on growth-dominated municipal planning processes. Transportation analysts unhappily forecast a doubling of the capacity of existing freeways and even the addition of another deck to the Golden Gate Bridge unless people began using alternative to automobiles.

Next the attendees were asked what alternatives were possible, at which point the outlook brightened considerably. Practical examples of many positive choices already exist in communities scattered throughout the Bay Area. If all of the potential alternatives were happening at optimum levels in every city and town, the decline of the region could be halted and actually turned around.

* * *

A Green City Program for San Francisco Bay Area Cities and Towns is a full account of all the areas of sustainability that were covered in the meetings. To illustrate the way beneficial changes could occur, a "Fable," usually based in some part on an actual occurrence, is related (these are set in San Francisco but transferable to anywhere else). Pictures of how urban areas could look and other outcomes that might result if the proposals were carried out are presented as "...in Green City: what's possible?"

The real heart of the Green City Program lies in the section headed "What can cities do to promote...?" Here the values and practices of a new kind of urban resident are matched with needed alterations in municipal policies to create a more livable future. Transforming the outlooks of people alone won't be enough to do the job; there must also be changes in city administrations to reflect self-reliant values. Cities and towns that are serious about sustainability can carry out significant large-scale public projects (refitting all municipal building to use some form of renewable energy, for instance) while also encouraging extra-governmental changes.

The popular will that can move governments in this direction can be generated through activist groups who organize Green City programs for their own communities. Invitations to join the program's planning process shouldn't be restricted to previously active veterans, but should include a wide range of interested people. These days most individuals, citizen organizations, businesses and labor groups are aware of urban decline and care strongly about some aspects of sustainability. Under a Green City umbrella, they can begin to care about all of them.

Green City groups can develop a platform for change that is most appropriate for their particular city or town. Once a platform is made public, it will become a powerful tool for influencing boards of supervisors, town councils, elected officials and candidates for office. (How can they explain *not* endorsing a Green City?) Local initiatives and bond issues could be drafted so that voters would have an opportunity to show their support and approve carrying out specific proposals. Eventually, Green City groups could link together to carry out bioregion-wide initiatives that aren't currently possible because of the separation of county jurisdictions.

The San Francisco Bay Area has been a leader in arousing ecological consciousness. Its residents have rallied to preserve natural features and oppose despoliation of the earth in ways that inspire people in the rest of North America and throughout the world. If we will now begin to establish well-rooted Green City programs, by the twenty-first century we can create a model that will save this great Pacific Basin life-place and show a positive direction that others can follow to rescue their part of the planet.

Peter Berg
Director, Planet Drum Foundation

References

1. Lester R. Brown and Jodi L. Jacobson, *The Future of Urbanization: Facing the Ecological and Economic Restraints*, Worldwatch Paper #77 (Washington, Worldwatch Institute, 1987).

2. Robert W. Fox, *The World's Urban Explosion*, National Geographic Volume 166, Number 2 (Washington, National Geographic Society, 1984).

3. *Projections '87* (Oakland, Association of Bay Area Governments, 1987).

Urban Planting

CHAPTER ONE

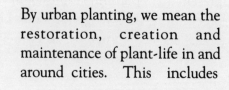

The way things are now

Cities needn't be monotonous carpets of concrete and buildings—places such as Barcelona, with its tree-lined central promenade, are proof of that. Yet the Northern California urban landscape has been increasingly defoliated over the past few decades. Large tracts of forest and grassland have been paved and built upon; street trees have fallen victim to neglect in the aftermath of Proposition 13, and trees that have died of old age have not always been replaced. These ecological insults and swaths of ugliness are not a necessary part of urban development: they are easily avoided or redressed. A city's buildings can be architectural marvels, but the city will look inaccessible and drab if there are few trees, parks or little natural landscaping to relieve an endless march of skyscrapers and identical stucco boxes. With proper attention, cities will be greener, and because of that literally more livable.

What do we mean by urban planting?

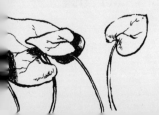

By urban planting, we mean the restoration, creation and maintenance of plant-life in and around cities. This includes

1

parks, median strips, sidewalk and rooftop planters, community and private gardens and vacant lots. It includes shade and fruit trees, vegetable patches, grasslands and scrub or chaparral. Sound urban planting practice includes a significant proportion of native vegetation, because natives require less maintenance and water than exotic counterparts, and provide places for native birds and animals to live.

What benefits can cities reap from urban planting?

- *More livable cities.* Cities typically devote almost all of their land area to buildings and streets. That's an impoverishing choice—aesthetically, physically and spiritually. Trees, bushes and grasslands are beautiful, and complement the beauty of Northern California's human artifacts. They can relieve the barrenness of the concrete and asphalt that cover much of the city. They provide shade when it's hot and shelter from winter storms and windy summer afternoons. Finally, people feel better in a setting that includes the natural as well as the manufactured.

- *Improved drainage.* Properly planted land absorbs the rain that falls on it, eliminating excessive run-off that now requires drainage with expensive storm sewers that often overflow and flood.

- *Closer-knit communities.* Sidewalk planting projects present an opportunity for residents to work together on bettering their neighborhoods. Unified neighborhoods are less vulnerable to crime, litter and other problems of urban blight.

What can cities do to promote urban planting?

Here are a few practical ideas for municipal policies that can be undertaken immediately to promote urban planting:

- Repeal ordinances and procedures that stand in the way of the literal greening of the cities (e.g., those that impede the planting of street trees and sidewalk strips), and codes that discourage or prohibit the planting of native species or of fruit trees in appropriate locations.

- Establish a consortium of the several municipal agencies and private groups that deal with urban planting to coordinate their efforts.

- Provide technical assistance and advice on tree care to residents who want to plant trees on their streets (for instance, jackhammers and operators to break up concrete sidewalks), and offer saplings and appropriate tools to such groups.

- Offer, sponsor or subsidize classes in urban gardening, and publish or fund a city directory of urban gardens and gardeners.

- Make available some city park land for citizen planting and gardening; plant fruit trees in parks and maintain them as public orchards.

3

• Investigate the use of the California Conservation Corps and the San Francisco Conservation Corps as a labor force for the planting of median strips, sidewalk-side strips, etc., being careful not to use them as a substitute for neighborhood involvement.

Longer-term visions for municipal action

• Assist in the establishment of local composting centers to collect kitchen scraps and plant trimmings from those who don't want them for their own compost. Make the compost available to parks and gardens in the city.

• Require developers to set aside a certain percentage of the area of their developments as plantable space, in sunny yards, in rooftop and window planter boxes and in sidewalk strips.

• Make city money available to neighborhood associations, homeowners or renters for urban revegetation and tree-planting, in the form of either tax incentives or a district levy.

• Encourage the growth of local commons, either by offering incentives to landowners to donate or grant long-term leases on plantable vacant lots, or by acquiring land and making it available to local residents (e.g., community control over "vest-pocket" parks). The large vegetable gardens in San Francisco's Fillmore District were a good example of such a commons while they existed.

Related fields

Urban Wild Habitat
A complementary need in Bay Area cities and towns is habitat for wild plants and animals. These suggestions for enhanced greening of the cities can be balanced with the preservation and restoration of wild places within and immediately surrounding cities.

A fable

Mrs. Wong was amazed by how much fruit her kids could go through in a week. It had been three years since her husband's death when they had moved into the small flat on a treeless street on lower Russian Hill. When her neighbors suggested a tree-planting for one weekend in March, she was happy to join in. After consultation with a city forester who spoke over tea at their evening meeting, the group settled on a combination of peaches, plums and cherries. They even threw in a lychee nut tree. A couple of days before the appointed weekend, workers from the city Public Works Department broke up the cement with jackhammers to get the residents started. They left behind a dumpster, some soil, stakes and a bale of chicken wire, and dropped off a few picks, shovels, and hoses at the Wongs' flat. On Saturday the forester showed up with the saplings, and twenty neighbors turned out to chuck chunks of cement into the

dumpster, dig the holes, set the young trees in them and protect them from dogs and other hazards with wire and stakes. The neighbors finished the day with an enormous banquet of dishes from half the provinces in China. Now the families take turns watering the trees, and have scheduled a day to clean up the vacant lot on their block to turn it into a vegetable garden. Their most ambitious upcoming project is to open up adjoining backyards in the middle of the block where they'll build a large greenhouse to grow vegetables and herbs.

Urban planting in Green City: what's possible?

In Green City, trees and other plants flourish where there used to be only concrete. Streets are planted with various tree species, most of them native to the region. Vacant lots have been leased and donated for community vegetable patches, and market gardens provide a good living for young entrepreneurs. Median strips have been replanted in native scrub and grasses, and now require virtually no maintenance. Fruit trees flourish in city parks, and families spend late summer afternoons picking the apples and pears. As the city grows greener, people start to look for new space to plant. Their attention is soon drawn to their own streets, many of which are far wider than the ever-diminishing traffic warrants. After a simple permit process, a city truck chews up a lane, hauls away the asphalt, drops off some new soil, and leaves the local residents to do the rest.

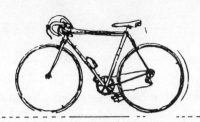

Smart Transportation

CHAPTER TWO

The way it is now

The transportation systems of most large cities are under serious stress. Freeway congestion and gridlock are endemic to the Bay Area and affect ever-larger regions for increasing portions of the day. Not only is it becoming difficult to get anywhere, but the neighborhood character of cities is being destroyed in the process. Busy, trafficked streets are inhospitable to pedestrians and to businesses that require foot-traffic to draw customers. With better transportation, getting where we need to go will be more congenial, and the current system's negative effects—pollution, noise and land waste—will be reduced.

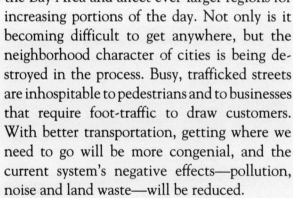
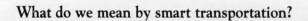

What do we mean by smart transportation?

Smart transportation means seeking appropriate, ecologically sound solutions to people's transportation needs, instead of trying to solve them all with more asphalt and single-occupancy vehicles. It means using a combination of techniques—such as self-propelled transit (foot and bicycle), buses, ride-sharing and proximity (working and playing near home)—to complement the role of the automobile, and giving preference to techniques such as cycling and walking that promote human-scale interactions and do not contribute to air or noise pollution.

What benefits can cities gain from smart transportation?

- *More workable cities.* Decreased use of automobiles in favor of more attractive alternatives will mean less noise, cleaner air and unclogged roads. It will mean less disruption to neighborhoods that now are bisected by streams of arterial traffic. More walking and cycling make for more face-to-face interaction between people and for fewer traffic injuries.

- *Decreased dependence on imported energy.* Motor vehicles consume a large fraction of the fossil fuels used in Bay Area cities and leave us vulnerable to price hikes and gas shortages. Smart transportation makes use of fuel-thrifty techniques that reduce those dangers and holds the promise of eventual reliance on fuel made from locally available biomass.

- *Reduced municipal expenditures.* Decreased traffic cuts highway maintenance costs, damage from accidents and fuel charges. New developments that incorporate smart transportation principles can slash infrastructure costs by narrowing roads and using more land for people, less for streets and related services.

What can cities do to promote smart transportation?

Here are a few suggestions for municipal policies that can be undertaken immediately:

• Levy a local gasoline tax, higher parking taxes and an auto tax (possibly based on Blue Book value divided by fuel economy) to help fund public transit, compensating for subsidies to auto transit (e.g., freeway construction and maintenance).

• Create auto-free pedestrian malls in dense sections of town to encourage foot traffic and to prevent congestion and parking problems. Where necessary, allow access by commercial vehicles at restricted hours.

• Install bike racks on some buses and allow bikes on trains to facilitate the bike-to-mass-transit connection and reduce the need for parking and shuttles at transit stations.

• Require developers to shoulder some of the transportation costs generated by their development (for instance, by coordinating vanpools or providing shuttles to commuter rail).

• Adopt mixed-use zoning policies to enable dwellings, workplaces and places of entertainment to be near each other for access by proximity instead of transportation; discourage housing-only subdivisions, commuter suburbs and urban sprawl.

- Promote services such as car- and vanpooling, which require low capital investment and offer high flexibility. (For example, provide tax incentives to employers to organize vanpools for their workers or to offer cash bonuses to employees who use ridesharing).

- Greatly expand facilities for cyclists, such as racks, lanes and off-street paths.

- Coordinate local transit scheduling with that of surrounding transit districts, for better transfers and connections between systems.

Longer-term visions for municipal action

- Reduce the width of all but arterial streets and their maximum speed limits to make the streets more hospitable to pedestrians and cyclists.

- Design some streets to include cul-de-sacs connected by bike paths, thus making the bicycle a swifter vehicle than the automobile in many instances (as was done in the Village Homes development in Davis, California).

- Speed transit trips by giving transit separate rights of way and the ability to pre-empt traffic signals; instituting an honor system for fares (passengers are on their honor to buy a ticket from a machine or hold a valid pass, enforcement is by random inspection and

fine) as is done is Europe and Portland, Oregon; and offering limited stop and express services on major arteries.

Related fields

Land use planning
Patterns of settlement in which people live near where they work and play can reduce the need for transportation services. See the proposals in Sustainable Planning for details.

A fable

The third time Mrs. Yuan was almost run over, she was hopping mad. The light had just turned green, and she stepped off the curb to cross Stockton Street. Just then, a pick-up truck roared into the intersection and through the red light, honking as it narrowly missed Mrs. Yuan's shopping bag and a couple of cars crossing its path. That night, she started wondering why cars needed to be on Stockton Street at all. As she pointed out to her family, Stockton Street serves the same purpose as the market in her home city of Guangdong, where their family had visited four years earlier. Even if delivery trucks did sometimes drive into the market, they certainly didn't whiz through. Pedestrians dominated the street, she argued—why not on Stockton? Her teenage son protested that he liked to cruise there with his buddies on Friday and Saturday nights, so she said, "OK, you can have the street in the evening, but I want it during the day." Mrs. Yuan talked up the idea to a couple of merchants she shopped from, and convinced them that people would come there more often if there weren't so many cars and so much exhaust. With their support in bringing the idea to other shopkeepers up and down the street, it wasn't long before their coalition was able to convince the Board of Supervisors to make the street, from Sacramento to Columbus Avenue, a pedestrian mall from 11 a.m. to 7 p.m. every day. Deliveries were made either before 11 a.m. or to the rear entrances that many stores already had off side streets. The Muni busdrivers happily took Powell Street instead of Stockton—without the double-parked vans and so on, they moved a lot more quickly. Business picked up so much that now, merchants in other parts of the city are pushing for the same thing.

Smart transportation in Green City: what's possible?

In Green City, the self-propelled and public transportation systems are so convenient that a lot of people have sold their cars. Sure, some folks have kept them to get out of the city on the weekends, but there's not much point to using them in town. All of the major streets have bicycle lanes or parallel bike paths—an innovation that was incorporated in the conversion to one-way streets. Buses are a lot swifter and more frequent, thanks to the Muni's honor fare system, the remote controls that bus drivers use to change the traffic signals to their favor when they near an intersection, and the huge drop in the number of cars clogging the streets. The decline in driving is also a result of the uniform gasoline tax that the nine Bay Area counties levied to subsidize public transit—and to let people know what it really costs society when they drive

their cars. The money has funded a series of improve-ments, such as the conversion of the Peninsula CalTrain line to a light-rail system linked to the Muni Metro (instead of ending at a terminal in the warehouse district south of Market) and the purchase of bike-path rights of way.

Least dramatic, but possibly most important, people don't have to go as far any more to get where they need to go, because of a set of "proximity policies" incorporated into the Master Plan. The city abandoned the outmoded suburban ideal of segregating residential and commercial uses, and has used tax incentives to encourage them to mix—along with light industry, workshops, and services. It has become much more common to live within a 15- or 20-minute walk of work—such a short distance that it almost always takes longer to drive and park than it does to walk or bike—especially with the barriers to through traffic that most neighborhoods have erected. People spend less time stuck in traffic and can go home on their lunchbreak or visit their kids in daycare. Even though mobility is central to the American character, no one seems to miss sitting in traffic jams with overheating cars and tempers.

Sustainable Planning

CHAPTER THREE

The way it is now

Development in the San Francisco Bay Area (like most metropolitan regions in North America) hasn't taken into account the natural carrying capacity of the land— how many people it can support over the long term and in what patterns of settlement. As a result, problems have arisen, such as the conversion of vast tracts of productive agricultural land into low-density suburbs and the consequent importation of food from progressively greater distances, congestion of transportation arteries with attendant inconvenience and effects on air quality, redevelopment and gentrification of neighborhoods whose former character was an integral component of the diversity of cultures in the area. Sustainable planning can focus on these prospective problems before they arise, or conceive of ways to reduce their impact once they do.

What do we mean by sustainable planning?

Sustainable planning refers both to the process of planning and its focus. Good planning examines the overall, cumulative effects of proposed changes in land use, and judges them in the context of the region's natural features such as climate, watercourses, seismic history and animal and plant life-cycles. In addition, it is developed at the grassroots level with active citizen participation in setting the agenda and proposing policies.

What benefits can cities reap from sustainable planning?

• *Livability over the long term.* The prosperity of a region is rooted in the health of the ecosystems that support it—the land, the air and the water. Sustainable planning considers proposed development with a view to preserving and improving these systems. What would paving large tracts of the San Ramon Valley do to its micro-climate? What health effects (on humans and animals) stem from the use of pesticides in Golden Gate Park? Unless these questions are on the agenda, they are sure to be disregarded.

• *Reduced food costs.* While short-term economies may be realized through chemical farming and wetland filling, in the long run, these strategies will prove expensive if water must be purified before it can return to the Bay, if farm productivity drops because the soil is used up or if the organisms low on the food chain are crowded out and cannot support commercially valuable species such as crab or sea bass.

15

- *Improved community participation.* Just as neighborhood-level action involves people in setting the destiny of their own neighborhoods and thus gives them more of a sense of ownership and responsibility for their immediate surroundings (see the section on Neighborhood Character and Empowerment), sustainable planning involves people in the choices that determine the ecological functioning of their regions and thus brings home the effect of people's actions on their environment.

What can cities do to promote sustainable planning?

Here are some ideas for municipal action that could be put into practice right away:

- Establish a staff to serve as sustainable planning advocates. They would counterbalance powerful monied interests that exert pressure on the planning process. A model could be the Public Staff Division of the Public Utilities Commission, which acts as a ratepayer advocate before the commission in rate cases. They would help the general public find out about the planning process and make its voice heard.

- Actively solicit neighborhoods' visions of their futures through methods such as attitude and preference polls and well-publicized, ongoing town-hall-style meetings. Elicit people's thoughts on what constitutes appropriate density and carrying capacity for their neighborhood, as has been done in parts of Berkeley. (How much parking? What proportion of retail to residential space?)

- Emphasize a long-term, regional perspective in city planning. Develop information about potential effects on the entire region, not just on the area within a city's jurisdiction. Use that information in planning decisions. Examine the cumulative impact of development schemes, not just the incremental change resulting from each one. (Failure to do so is evident on the Peninsula, where each of several dozen Bayshore developments had a small effect on traffic, but taken together, have attracted more cars than Highway 101 can handle.)

- Discourage or prohibit the conversion of valuable agricultural land into low-density suburbs that require a high investment in roads and city services and increase dependency on the automobile. Promote instead "proximity policies" that encourage people to live near their workplaces.

- Identify "sacred places" (ranging from parks to landmark buildings to cafés and teen hangouts) that may not be removed or disturbed.

- Illustrate and celebrate the community's ideals about livability by underwriting the construction of exemplary and unique buildings and public spaces; develop a guide to instances in which planning for livability has succeeded (such as St. Francis Square in San Francisco).

- Raise citizen awareness of the elements, techniques and importance of sustainable practices (such as recycling and urban planting), using a variety

17

of media in order to reach a broad cross-section of the population. Include such points as the benefits of high-density living, the relationship between city and country, and the need for open space and wild habitat within urban areas.

Longer-term visions for municipal action

• Adopt "statutes of responsibility" that delineate the obligations of officials and agencies to preserve the health of the city and its inhabitants, and that require developers to internalize costs generated by their development and currently imposed on the public. These range from water and sewer use to air pollution and encroachment on open space.

• Heavy traffic disrupts street life and destroys neighborhoods. Wherever possible, reverse cars' domination of the landscape, recapture land devoted to the automobile (sometimes approaching 60 percent of urban land area) for other uses, and restrict the allocation of more land to car-related use.

• As a way to reduce urban sprawl, use city money to buy, move or demolish buildings that are located in ecologically sensitive or valuable areas (e.g., along waterfront, creeks or hilltops) and are near the end of their useful lives.

Related fields

Many of the proposals described in other elements of this platform can be advanced through appropriate zoning policies and all should be considered in light of their impact on the health of the entire region.

A fable

What finally got people riled up was the Fotomat. North Beach had been relatively unscathed by homogenizing chain stores like Burger King, Thrifty, and La Petite Boulangerie, so when word spread that the Bohemian Cigar Store's lease had been bought out by Fotomat, the neighbors were incensed. It was a good honest café, and North Beach had seemed like the final hold-out against the chains. A few days after the deal went down, word began to spread and Angela Spinelli started standing at the corner of Columbus and Union, passing out fliers that demanded, "Don't Shut the Cigar Box!" and invited people to a meeting at St. Peter and Paul's church on Washington Square. On meeting night, so many people showed up that the church ran out of chairs. The Cigar Store had become an institution, and they weren't going to let it go, or let this be a harbinger of things to come. The meeting catalyzed opposition to the quick-photo place.

They formed an action committee and got people down to City Hall to the hearing on the zoning variances that the developers were requesting. More than that, the meeting got people thinking about figuring out an overall vision for the neighborhood so that they, their kids, and their grandkids wouldn't always have to go to City Hall to keep the neighborhood from being invaded by homogeneous non-culture. Angela passed out more fliers at the City Hall hearing and at the rally that the committee held in Washington Square among the T'ai Chi artists. They launched a participative project they called "Envisioning North Beach: Our Neighborhood in the year 2010." Now the

19

participants—from all the ethnicities in the district, representing different age groups and all levels of affluence—are figuring out what they want their neighborhood to be like in the years ahead, and how to get there.

Sustainable planning in Green City: what's possible?

In Green City, the sprawl that once characterized the metropolitan region has been replaced by more thoughtful use of land. Cities such as San Francisco and Oakland have adapted better to high densities; and low-density uses (such as suburbs) have gradually vanished, replaced instead by small towns surrounded by open space of various sorts—agricultural land, parks and wildlife preserves. Each town contains a mixture of different uses: houses and apartments, service businesses, light industry and entertainment. Though it's small enough that no place in it is more than a 20-minute walk from the countryside, within the town there's a lot of greenery—streetside gardens, creeks, and public orchards. It's big enough to support a couple of movie theaters, a couple dozen restaurants, a few bakeries, and so on. Most people's houses are in the same town as their workplace, so commuting is greatly reduced. That doesn't mean that the towns are isolated islands, though. They're linked by swift light rail systems and bike paths that enable people to visit friends and take advantage of other towns' specialties without hassle or the use of single-passenger automobiles.

Renewable Energy

CHAPTER FOUR

The way things are now

At present, cities depend heavily on energy sources—oil, coal, nuclear power—that pollute the air and water and are generally projected to become scarcer and more expensive. U.S. oil will last only until 2015, at current rates of extraction. In addition, fossil fuel use exposes cities to the specter of energy cut-offs caused by accident, sabotage, natural disaster, and geopolitical conflict continents away. These vulnerabilities are easily reduced by using energy more efficiently and by shifting to renewable energy sources such as solar power, hydropower, wood, and wind energy.

What do we mean by renewable energy?

Fossil fuels such as oil and gas come from finite reserves created by the decay of plants over millions of years, which cannot be regenerated on a human time-scale. In contrast,

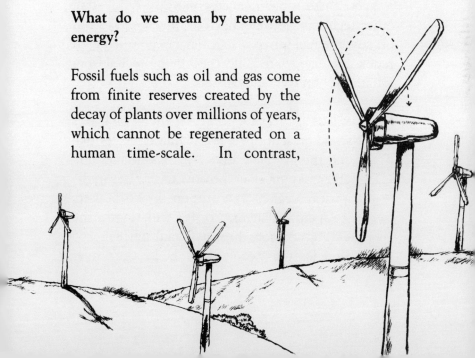

renewable energy sources come from natural flows in the environment, such as sunlight and falling water. If designers take into account fluctuations in weather and climate, these flows are consistent and dependable enough to serve as reliable energy sources. Coupled with improvements in the efficiency of all energy use, renewable sources can supply all of a city's energy needs.

What benefits can cities gain from renewable energy?

- *Reduced pollution.* Renewable energy technology produces much less pollution than do conventional sources. Air, water and land will be more life-supporting than they are now for generations to come.

- *Lower energy costs.* The first prerequisite for smart energy use is improving the efficiency with which we use energy. Conservation costs a fraction of the price of a kilowatt-hour or gallon of gasoline. The next cheapest energy strategy is conversion to renewable sources: these sometimes cost more to build than other technologies, but they cost much less to run because the fuel is free. Once devices powered with renewable energy are built, they are protected from inflation, shortages, and cut-offs.

- *Improved base of local jobs.* Money spent on oil leaves the city and enriches people in faraway places like Texas and the Middle East. With renewables and energy efficiency, much of the work takes place in the communities or regions where the energy is to be used, so money spent on energy keeps circulating in the area, creating more jobs through a "multiplier effect." (For example, the people who build your solar greenhouse spend their wages at local restaurants, barbershops and grocery stores.)

What can cities do to promote renewable energy?

Here are a few practical ideas for municipal policies that could be undertaken immediately to promote the transition to renewable energy:

Help people find out what works

- Set an example of smart energy use by demonstrating applications of energy efficiency and renewable energy in municipal buildings, such as libraries, schools and firehouses. For instance, city offices can be equipped with better fluorescent light ballasts, which cut energy consumption 40 percent and eliminate the lights' annoying flicker and hum. Such improvements will pay for themselves out of energy savings, and could be financed with revenue bonds under that premise.

- Sponsor energy education programs, displays on renewable energy (at libraries, schools, neighborhood centers and the Exploratorium), and the distribution of information, by either city staff or city-funded community groups. Orient these programs to look beyond glut-and-shortage cycles to the next 10, 20 or 40 years.

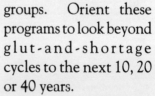

  - Make a more vigorous effort to reach low-income households eligible for free weatherization through existing groups such as the Economic Opportunity Council. Assign other community human-service departments to educate and inform all households about energy efficiency. Consider using money from utilities to finance such improvements.

Remove existing barriers

• Pass ordinances requiring that homes and apartments be weatherized when sold (as has been done in San Francisco, Berkeley and elsewhere) or by a certain deadline (as have been done in Portland).

• Find out if and how building codes impede the use of solar and other renewable energy sources. Revise restrictions for renewables where appropriate (for instance, allow solar collectors to exceed normal building height limits by up to 10 feet, allow solar green-houses smaller setbacks than other structures) and streamline other requirements (as Berkeley has done for solar water heater permits).

Longer-term visions for municipal action

• Encourage the installation of utility meters that are more useful to the general public, showing the dollar-cost of energy as well as raw consumption data.

• Consider the energy potential of municipal discards, including the conversion of sewage to methane gas (which runs Modesto's municipal car fleet), provided that environmental quality and recycling options are not compromised.

• Where practical, collect yard and park clippings for processing into liquid or gaseous fuels such as alcohol and methane. Provide for separate pickup of this plant material where warranted. Cycle leftover mash into composting and fertilizer operations.

• Research new ways in which natural processes, like photosynthesis, can be used to supply the region's energy needs. Develop a plan for eventual implementation of those strategies.

Related fields

Transportation
Motor vehicles consume a large fraction of the energy used in Bay Area cities, besides having substantial environmental impact and degrading the quality of life. The proposal on Smart Transportation examines some ways of reconciling our needs for mobility with the cost of automobiles in terms of livability.

Land-use planning
Patterns of settlement in which people live near their work and entertainment can reduce the need for transportation and thus reduce energy consumption. See the proposal on Sustainable Planning for details.

A fable

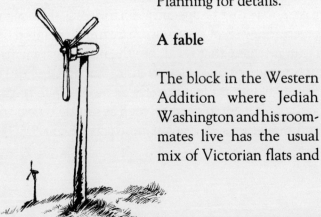

The block in the Western Addition where Jediah Washington and his roommates live has the usual mix of Victorian flats and more recent but nonetheless very San Franciscan dwellings. Most of the buildings were poorly insulated, but last fall, Jediah decided he was tired of having his living room seem colder than Alamo Square. He talked to his neighbors at church, and they decided to band together and fix up their houses for the winter. They ordered weatherstripping, attic insulation and caulk in bulk, and convinced the dealers to give them a good price for the stuff. Then the city paid for a couple of people who had some experience to show them how to apply weatherstripping to the door and window frames. The workers taught Jediah and his neighbors to use caulk guns, and they insulated Mother Robinson's attic to demonstrate how it was done. It was a lot of work, but it sure paid off on January mornings, and Jediah's share of his household's heating bill is running about half what it had been. They've gotten a good work crew together, and are making plans for solar greenhouses to build in the spring.

Energy in Green City: what's possible?

In Green City, almost all of the energy services (warmth, mobility, lighting, power, etc.) are provided through the efficient use of renewable resources. Homes have been weatherstripped, insulated and fit with windows to warm the rooms with sunlight. Wind machines are mounted in passes between hilltops outside of town where the summer breezes blow. Biological sewage treatment plants produce clean methane that is fed into the natural gas mains and rich fertilizer that is delivered to farmers near the city. Fewer people drive automobiles alone—public transit and its companion systems (such as shuttle buses, jitneys and shared taxis) are much more convenient.

Winners and Losers

People who pay utility bills are big winners in the transition to renewable energy—their bills are cut in half. Everyone benefits from cleaner air and water, and everyone is spared the fear that is part of living with the threat of nuclear accidents and oil spills. Some dislocation may occur as the number of jobs in the fossil fuel industry declines—but many of those people can be retrained and taught skills that are more appropriate to the way of energy in Green City. Utilities and fossil fuel companies may find that their assets are worth less. But many farsighted utilities have already diverted resources into the development and use of renewable energy, and have begun the switch—ARCO is a major manufacturer of solar cells, and both Southern California Edison and PG&E emphasize renewable energy in their strategic plans.

Neighborhood Character
and Enpowerment

CHAPTER FIVE

The way it is now

Cities are too large and anonymous to offer the sense of community and belonging that builds a stable society.

The neighborhood, on the other hand, is a unit that people can identify with more easily—in which it's possible to know some of the local families, the storekeepers, the bars and cafés, the auto mechanics— and where different ethnic groups can accumulate the critical mass they need to maintain cultural life. For these benefits to appear, people must have enough control over the place to feel it is truly their own.

What do we mean by neighborhood character and empowerment?

Neighborhood character is the flavor of the place, including such diverse elements as the architecture, the topography, the language on commercial signs, the forms of religious worship, the family structure—in short, the culture of the place. It's an expression of the unique combination of people who have settled in a particular area. Often a neighborhood such as Chinatown, the Latin Mission District or Italian North Beach, is influenced by its people's ethnic background. Neighborhood empowerment is the process by which the people who live in a neighborhood gain and exercise the right to make informed decisions about issues that affect the place in which they live, such as the types of new development that will be permitted, traffic and parking arrangements, and so on.

What benefits can cities reap from neighborhood character and empowerment?

- *A more stable city.* The more people identify with their neighborhood, the more likely they are to stay there a long time. Neighborhoods with character are more attractive to most people than graceless speculator-built tracts.

- *Safer neighborhoods.* The more stable the area, the more people get to know each other and the more they can look out for each other. If you know your neighbors, you know whether that moving truck is really there to move the Yamamotos' belongings to New Jersey, or whether there's something fishy going on.

- A *cleaner city*. The longer people's tenure in a place, and the more control they have over it, the more they treat it like their own, and the less likely they are to litter or deface it.

- *Tourist drawing power*. Neighborhoods that express a unique ethnic flavor can draw travelers who want to see how other subcultures within the country live. Such is the case with Chinatown and North Beach, and to a lesser extent with other neighborhoods in the city.

What can cities do to promote neighborhood character and empowerment?

These are a few municipal policies that could be undertaken right away:

- Foster the formation of Neighborhood Design Review Boards, to act as representatives of the neighborhood in the planning process. Require developers to incorporate in their plans recommendations from these boards. Require the construction of community facilities and the adoption of human-scale design, like the Mission Creek Conservancy plan recommends for Mission Bay in San Francisco.

- Fund neighborhood-scale activities and institutions such as "commons areas" and meeting places where people in each neighborhood can help carry out local projects and organize and represent the community on larger issues. These staffers should be hired by and accountable to the neighborhood organization.

- Broaden neighborhood representation on Police Community Relations Boards, and use the boards as vehicles to define what constitutes the appropriate exercise of police power in individual neighborhoods. (Neighborhood self-patrol may be more appropriate in many cases.)

• Create a municipal agency to act as an advocate for neighborhood and non-developer views on aspects of transportation and land-use issues. Develop mechanisms such as district elections to improve the representation of neighborhoods in the municipal decision-making process.

• Establish a fund to help low-income people pay rental deposits and avoid eviction, in order to preserve the diversity and stability of the city's population. Money for the fund could be raised from the hotel tax, for instance. Emphasize keeping existing housing affordable as well as constructing new affordable housing by controlling rent increases on vacant housing units and small commercial space.

• Encourage local celebrations such as street fairs and Carnival as a way to strengthen connections among neighborhood residents and to express the cultural diversity of the city.

Related fields

Sustainable planning
Urban planning can promote features that will make neighborhoods more livable—such as keeping through streets from bisecting neighborhoods, low-rise construction, and unobtrusive parking (no 3-acre parking lots).

A fable

The McCoppin family lives in a stucco house on Bernal Heights. They knew when they bought the place that there was a church on the block, but it wasn't until they had been there for a few weeks that they realized what a parking problem it presented. It wasn't just the Sunday worship service—it was the bingo nights and the fact that the church served as a community center for its congregation. The parking lot was too small to meet the demand, so the cars of the faithful spilled out onto the sidewalk, and the church employed an attendant to choreograph the movement of autos in and out.

The McCoppins were willing to tolerate that, but a year later when the church elders became set on buying out a few nearby houses and tearing them down to make way for more Toyotas, the family sprang into action. They dropped off a letter at the other houses on the block and followed up in door-to-door conversations; when they arranged a hearing at City Hall, an impressive four dozen people turned out to protest the proposed demolitions. After they defeated the church's bid to rezone the area in question for parking, they realized that for the first time in recent memory, the neighborhood was organized. The McCoppins called a meeting of the people on their block and the few surrounding ones, and formed an ongoing association to consider new construction in their neighborhood and offer suggestions to people who wanted to build there. Their ability to turn people out for hearings downtown has actually given those suggestions a fair bit of persuasive force with developers; even the church elders have become a bit more conciliatory. They are now looking into other ways of making their neighborhood more livable, such as speed bumps, traffic barriers, and neighborhood watch and conflict resolution, so the police don't have to be called as often.

Neighborhoods in Green City: what's possible?

The city is divided into scores of neighborhoods of several thousand people each. Neighborhood councils sprang up in the 1990s, in response to the city's offer of "home rule" for neighborhoods that could form a duly elected assembly of five or more people to represent their views. The neighborhood reps don't get much of a chance to stray out of line, since they see their constituents tending their gardens and shopping at the corner store. As time went by and the councils proved their worth, they gained more control over their turf—first just variances from zoning codes, then traffic, local parks, and bus routes. Most have working groups to mediate disputes among neighbors, and many have set up local patrols to keep the streets safe at night—people sign up for a night a month to spend a couple of hours walking around with a neighbor, just checking things out. Funny thing is, the neighborhoods seem safer now, even though the police rarely come by—parents aren't afraid to let their kids play in the street, and in many places no one can remember the last time someone was mugged.

Recycling and Reuse

CHAPTER SIX

The way it is now

Cities are notoriously prolific producers of garbage. Every day, a convoy of semi-trailer trucks carries San Francisco's refuse to Altamont Pass—a longer haul than most people commute to work. Those trucks contain valuable resources that are being wasted, instead of helping to provide jobs for city-dwellers and generating income in the city. Recycling and reuse offer ways to make use of those resources, and at the same time reduce the drain that Bay Area cities put on the rural areas that supply their raw materials.

What do we mean by recycling and reuse?

Recycling and reuse mean salvaging discarded materials rather than burying or burning them. They may be used again in their original form (such as returnable bottles or old chairs or doors), reused for a different purpose (such as paper pressed into artificial logs), decomposed organically (such as the composting of kitchen scraps), or reprocessed (such as the recovery of the glass or metal content from bottles, aluminum cans or auto engines). Good discard practice calls for making the best and highest use of what is discarded: reuse is more efficient than recycling, for example, because processing a bottle for refilling takes less energy than making a whole new bottle.

What benefits can cities reap from recycling and reuse?

- *Lower city costs.* Recycling and reuse programs offer an economical way for cities to dispose of their discards while paying lower disposal fees. Because they salvage value from the supply of discards, recycling and reuse programs can reduce the necessity and cut the costs of dumping garbage in landfills, while generating income from the products people want to dispose of.

- *More job opportunities.* Recycling programs generate a large part of their own revenues, supporting their own employees. They also create jobs by helping to expand small and large shops and plants that recondition reusable goods or process recyclable materials into new products. Since landfills and other garbage technologies create few jobs, recycling technologies displace few workers and result in a net increase in employment.

- *More stable garbage costs.* As cities run out of nearby landfill sites, they are forced to haul their garbage farther away. This process results in escalating costs for refuse dumping. Recycling and reuse programs prolong the life of existing sites, and reduce the total volume that must be transported there.

- *Reduced pressure on wilderness resources.* Recycling cuts the demand for "first-run" materials that are typically brought from rural areas to the city, such as wood fiber (in the form of paper or particle board) and primary metals. Composting also makes it possible to return the nutrients from kitchen scraps and yard trimmings to the soil, either in the city or where the food was grown. (Imagine the amount of compost that the kitchens of San Francisco's 740,000 residents could produce, along with their garden clippings, tree-trimmings, etc.)

- *Elimination of the need for incineration.* Waste incineration is an old technology, but as implemented today has high capital and environmental costs. Burning garbage turns the air, instead of the land, into a garbage dump. Its primary attraction is the illusion it creates that garbage goes away. With serious recycling, the waste stream won't be big enough to justify an incinerator.

What can cities do to promote recycling and reuse?

Here are a few municipal policies that could be undertaken right away to promote recycling and reuse:

- Make it easier for residents and businesses to recycle instead of wasting discards—institute curbside pickup of separated recyclables, provide or sell special containers for materials to be recycled, and modify city street cans to allow material separation.

• Encourage the design and construction of transfer stations that give priority to recycling and to processing separate streams of materials.

• Establish an ongoing municipal recycling working group to study the composition of the solid waste stream, define what constitutes recycling, measure the amount of recycling underway, set disposal fees, and monitor recycling contracts.

• Buy recycled materials for municipal use as a way of creating markets for recyclables. For example, city governments could purchase recycled paper for all its duplicating and word processing to help establish that industry.

• Raise tonnage fees for landfill disposal to encourage the recycling of high-volume, low-value materials such as brush, concrete and mixed paper; offer an alternative to the flat monthly home garbage can fee that charges according to the volume actually thrown away, such as the specially printed garbage bags used in Holland, Michigan, whose purchase price includes the cost of disposal.

• Establish the cost per ton that recycling saves the city com-pared to landfill disposal and apply the difference to support the expansion of recycling. The savings could be collected by charging higher garbage collection rates or landfill gate-fee surcharges.

• Encourage the establishment of secondary-materials industries in or near the city through such means as tax incentives and loan guarantees.

Longer-term visions for municipal action

• Tax difficult-to-recycle packaging to account for the cost of disposal that its use will impose on the city, or ban certain kinds of packaging (such as Los Angeles has done with foamed plastics) altogether.

• Collect kitchen scraps and yard trimmings and redistribute or compost them at neighborhood composting centers. Careful pasteurization of food scraps can make them safe for animal feed. The centers could provide organic fertilizer to nearby parks and community gardens, lessening the use of chemicals.

Related fields

Renewable energy
Recycling saves on the energy required to manufacture something from scratch.

A fable

Cuong Nguy was outraged. When he arranged for a dumpster for the renovation job he and his friends were doing in the Richmond, he learned that the cost of renting one had just tripled. The clerk on the other end was very patient, explaining that the whole city was now facing the same higher charges. The old charges hadn't covered the city's costs, and it finally decided to stop subsidizing people for throwing things away. Cuong could understand that, but he was still outraged. He muttered about all of these frustrations to the guys who worked on his crew, as they heaved pieces of an old concrete patio floor into the dumpster, until one of them pointed out that he didn't have to throw the stuff away. "You know," Duoc Van Tham said, "my brother-in-law, Hoa, could probably use some of this stuff as backfill around the foundation he's putting in." Duoc called him up, and sure enough, Hoa came by a couple of days later in a flatbed to load up with what looked like worthless rubble to Cuong but was valuable fill to Hoa.

The incident got Cuong to thinking about the real meaning of waste. Within a few weeks, he had put up signs around town offering to dispose cheaply of various kinds of sorted discards, offering at the same time to sell various low-grade commodities-brush, wood waste, old bricks and reinforced concrete. In effect, he had set himself up as a materials broker, and it wasn't long before he was doing a roaring business.

Recycling and reuse in Green City: what's possible?

In Green City, the crude garbage cans of the 1980s are a thing of the past. In their place are sophisticated containers, each with several compartments: for tin, glass, cardboard, newspaper, a couple of grades of paper and miscellany. Aluminum cans

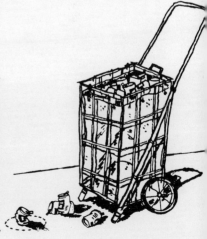

have practically vanished, in the wake of deposit legisla-
tion that made it more economical to supply beverages in
refillable bottles; most glass is reused because of those
laws. The primitive garbage trucks of the past have been
replaced by more elegant models with multiple compartments to match those on the household recycling
containers. Household kitchen scraps are set out
separately and picked up by a fellow who lives on the
block. He collects the stuff in a hand-drawn wagon. Some
of it he feeds to his chickens; the rest he composts (along
with the chicken manure) in bins in the community
garden. For these services he draws a small stipend from
the city, which pays him out of the disposal fees from the
block. The neighbors then use the compost on their
vegetable plots, and enjoy the benefit of the rich humus
without the task of shoveling their kitchen scraps in with
straw and soil.

Celebrating Life-Place Vitality

CHAPTER SEVEN

The way it is now

When people experience the vitality of natural features, the awareness raises public consciousness and creates the "cultural glue" for carrying out a full Green City Program. Urban people often don't feel connected with natural systems and don't recognize what benefits healthy life-places can bring. Using the arts and media to celebrate and inform ourselves about the natural aspects of urban life reconnects people with life-places and deepens their appreciation of them. For example, knowing something about food chains in the Bay can stimulate people to want to restore animal habitat to its former richness. Increased awareness of the impact on aquatic life of street-surface chemicals and oil that flow through storm sewers, for example, will bring the community to action. Such techniques can make the Green City process more vibrant and exciting than dry policy-making.

41

What do we mean by "celebrating life-place vitality"?

Celebrating life-place vitality means recognizing and expressing regard for the unique natural features—native plants and animals, climate, seasonal variations, and many others—that mark the places where we live. Doing this through a variety of media and art forms is both rewarding as a creative effort and effective as a means of educating and activating the community.

What benefits can be gained from celebrating life-place vitality?

- *Beautiful cities and towns.* The presence of public art and events that show high regard for natural features of a place is appealing to both residents and visitors.

- *Improved public entertainment and recreational possibilities.* Outdoor sites for artworks and information about natural underpinnings offer opportunities to explore while learning more about this dimension of living in a city.

- A *sense of continuity and authenticity in urban life.* Publicly acknowledging natural vitality in urban areas makes people feel in tune with elements that are relatively changeless and enduring, and inspires creativity and deeper bioregional culture.

What can cities do to promote celebrating life-place vitality?

- Find more ways to acquire and present works of art (such as sculpture, murals, poetry, dance and music, among others) that express community identification with local natural features and characteristics. Stress depictions and descriptions of natural history in public libraries, museums and public art programs.

- Provide information to the general public on the original natural appearance and character of the sites where cities and towns now stand. In addition to conventional means such as booklets, displays and lectures, develop innovative approaches—on-site models and graphics, tours of the original bay shore, events celebrating equinoxes and solstices—that highlight life-place phenomena.

- Identify and celebrate animals and natural features that have endured intact despite urbanization, such as hawks on Twin Peaks, the natural vegetation still flourishing in Glen Park, estuaries tucked away from people's attention such as Mission Creek, and hills that have escaped quarriers and developers, such as the rocks above the Josephine P. Randall Junior Museum in the upper Haight. Create urban nature guides that describe what is unique about the bioregion and what plants, animals, climate, and other characteristics distinguish it.

- Assist in developing small-scale, localized media such as murals, neighborhood newsletters and radio shows, and community bulletin

boards. Showcase public artworks in places that are accessible to people in their daily lives. (For example, people walk through the Mission District's Balmy Alley to view murals painted on the walls, garage doors and fences lining its sides.)

A fable

Jack Marshall paused during brunch one Sunday to look out the window of the Upper Market Street apartment he shared with his lover, Tim. It was late March, and the warm weather had brought out a profusion of wildflowers on the slopes of Twin Peaks. Jack had just taken a workshop on native plants, and mentioned to their friends that Twin Peaks was the largest chunk of the Franciscan ecosystem left in the City.

No one had heard of a "Franciscan ecosystem," so Jack explained that it was the combination of plants and animals that lived on the northern Peninsula before the Europeans came—the lupine, poppy, bunchgrasses, foxes and so on—which used to cover the city. After a moment's silence, Tim commented that the coming of spring to that hillside was one of the highlights of his year—it represented more hope than all the political rallies you could count. For him, spring was really something for the community to celebrate.

His friends agreed, and they decided to organize a meadow fair on Twin Peaks to celebrate high spring wildflowers and all the rest. They sent out flyers asking people to come in costume as their favorite native plant or animal. Six months after Halloween, people were ready to dress up again, and they really did it up. Hawk costumes, poppy suits, fox get-ups, lupine hats—they were all there.

People from all over the Castro gathered on one of the knobs of Twin Peaks, mingling with the flora and the fauna. A couple of naturalists were on hand to give tours of the native plants in the area, and an artist helped people paint masks of various Franciscan personae. People had a great time, and there was even talk of making it an annual event.

Celebrating life-place vitality in Green City

In Green City, the turning of the season is an occasion for private notice and public celebration—the return of the salmon to the coastal creeks, the appearance of the first wildflowers, the first refreshing rains of fall. The lore of these cycles can be found not only between the covers of books, but on street corners and in alleyways in the form of murals, plaques, parades and street theater. Numerous vista points have displays of photographs and engravings that show that view decades or centuries earlier. Pop songs on the radio mark what's special, culturally and ecologically, about the city and the region. There has even been a proliferation of small record labels, radio stations, and so on, serving neighborhoods, particular communities, and ethnic groups.

Urban Wild Habitat

CHAPTER EIGHT

The way it is now

Cities, with their millions of human inhabitants, are obviously dominated by an artificial environment. But just as people enjoy bringing domesticated animals into their lives, so city-dwellers would benefit from the integration of wildlife and wild habitat into the urban environment. It will counteract the overwhelmingly human-controlled flavor of the city and make our surroundings a healthier, more balanced and appealing place to live.

What do we mean by urban wild habitat?

Urban wild habitat is a place for untamed animals to live within and around the metropolis. It includes parks, marshes, lagoons, estuaries and creeks where terns, coots, raccoons, squirrels and even deer might live; it can also include less obvious homes, such as peregrine falcon nests on the

46

ledges of high-rise buildings. It requires not only physical room for animals to live and roam but also freedom from harassment and enough territory to support the rest of the food chain that the animals depend on.

What benefits can cities gain from urban wild habitat?

- *Improved quality of life.* The presence of other species such as dogs and cats complements the human presence and enriches city-dwellers' experience. The existence of wild animals and their habitats nearby takes that enhancement several steps further, adding a deeper understanding of humanity's place in the web of life. The existence of urban wild habitat makes undomesticated animals a visible reality, especially for children, instead of just something to read about in books. It can bring back the spirit of St. Francis of Assisi, for whom the city was named.

- *An indicator of ecological health.* The vigor and robustness of these native animals and plants indicate how clean the air and water are, and can help us assess the health and life-supporting capacity of the entire ecosystem.

- *An awareness of the natural cycles of the life-place.* By having wildlife close at hand, city-dwellers can see how other species respond to the changing seasons. They can draw on the rhythms of those species to mark their year by events such as the rutting of the deer, the winter return of the salmon or the fall migration of the hawks, bringing them in closer touch with the natural systems of which they're a part.

• *Near by opportunities for sightseeing and outdoor activities.* A San Francisco that successfully combines a rich cosmopolitan environment with the presence of wildlife will be even more attractive to visitors than it already is. A healthy Bay at the heart of our region will invite anglers to pursue bass and sturgeon and share their catch with friends and family without fear of contamination. It will draw sea lions, harbor seals, and otters (already returned to Monterey Bay) to the protected waters of San Francisco Bay, with tourists and locals in tow. (Imagine watching from a pierside café table as sea lions frolic in the wake of the Larkspur Ferry.)

What can cities do to promote wild habitat?

Here are a few municipal policies that can be undertaken immediately:

• Re-examine all city activities with an eye to restraining the release of toxic chemicals (for example, insecticide use in parks or oily run-off from Muni garages) that risk poisoning urban plants and animals.

• Require development to stay a certain minimum distance (setback) from streambanks and marshlands, in order to preserve the unique habitat that occurs where water meets land. Take serious account of the existence of wild habitat in deciding whether to permit proposed development.

• Protect and restore wildlife habitat where possible within city limits (for instance, for deer or elk in large undeveloped parks; for peregrine falcons on the ledges of downtown buildings). Such set-asides should be minimum requirements for any developments that are approved (such as preservation of salt marsh habitat in Mission Bay).

- Establish mechanisms—for instance, tax check-offs, development taxes, toxic chemicals taxes, or bond issue—to fund the maintenance of existing urban wild habitat and the creation of new wild places.

- Create a Department of Natural Life, or a regular forum of concerned divisions of city agencies, to coordinate their efforts on behalf of urban wildness; to identify, restore, and protect areas of wildness. Involve citizens and naturalists in decisions regarding the use of public parks and open space.

- Educate citizens on a local level (by neighborhood or district) about the wild plants and animals in their immediate area in order to cultivate an appreciation of wildness. Encourage local grantmakers to fund neighborhood groups to conduct this kind of research and outreach. Education can take place in schools, libraries, and parks. For example, encourage teachers to develop courses in local biology and ecology beginning with first grade.

Longer-term visions for municipal action

- Establish corridors of wildness linking regions of wild habitat, so that animals' territories can be large enough to support viable, self-sustaining populations.

- Where possible, bring creeks and streams above ground from the storm drains where they have been confined by primitive methods of flood control. Such creeks could constitute the wild corridors mentioned and could be managed to become healthy riparian habitats which help control floods naturally by absorbing overflow.

Related fields

Urban planting
The planting of native species, described in the proposal on Urban Planting, can provide food and cover for wild animals, birds, reptiles and insects (such as the native monarch butterfly).

A fable

When Jesús Ruiz came home from fourth grade one day, he had a story that really caught his parents' imagination. His class was studying a unit called "Wild in the City" that described how San Francisco looked before the Spanish arrived. Jesús brought home a map with two versions of San Francisco: 1750s and 1980s, and he and his mother spread it out on the kitchen table, poring over it and figuring out what natural features lay near their Mission District home. Most surprising was that there had once been a lake at the bottom of what is now Dolores Park, at 18th and Dolores Streets, with a creek flowing down what is now 18th Street toward Mission Creek, north of Potrero Hill. That got them to thinking that a pond and stream would be great for the neighborhood. They talked it over with their neighbors, who liked the idea even if it was a little far-out. The staff at the Water Department told them that the stream was still there, flowing daily through the storm sewers. After a lot of doorbell-ringing in the neighborhood and meetings at Rec and Parks, they got a hearing one evening at Mission High School. The room was packed, and everyone spoke up for a pond in the park, with egrets and grebes and maybe even a couple of pairs of herons. So the bulldozers and trenchers started work on recreating the features that were there before the park was landscaped early in the century, using old photographs to guide them. The Ruizes are still working on bringing the stream above ground—they figure they'll make 18th Street a pedestrian mall first, and then no one will complain that the creek will take away their parking places. The ever-curious egrets have already started flying over to check out the pond-and-creek-in-progress.

Wild habitat in Green City: what's possible?

In Green City, you can set out in the morning from the Bay and walk on trails alongside creeks all the way up into the hills that are the spine of the city. The wetlands where the creeks empty into the Bay have been restored and a tremendous variety of waterfowl lives there—egrets, blue herons, marsh hawks and more. You can head upstream along creeks that have been brought above ground, and trace a hundred-foot-wide swath of green through the maze of asphalt and concrete. Most streets run on overpasses or viaducts over the streams, making it necessary only rarely to cross a street at the same level as the cars. The creekside vegetation has been restored, too—willows, alders, ferns and the minty yerba buena for which the city was named grow in profusion. Animals have returned to take their place in the city again; although the

grizzly bear is still gone, it is not uncommon on Islais Creek to come upon deer and foxes, or to look up and see a red-tailed hawk circling in pursuit of small rodents. Further up the creek, the park widens out in its original wildness; here, in May and June, you can see the Mission Blue and San Bruno Elfin butterflies that once verged on extinction. In January, when the rains are fiercest, people come to watch the salmon spawn in the headwaters of the Islais, doing their final dance as they mate and die. From the headwaters, the trails lead over the top of the hill to another creek that flows down Mt. Davidson and empties into Lake Merced. By mid-afternoon, at the end of the hike, you are near the zoo—and might go in if your appetite for encountering other species hadn't been satisfied by all of the real wild animals on the hike.

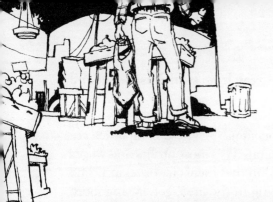

Socially Responsible Small Businesses and Cooperatives

CHAPTER NINE

The way it is now

Some large firms are so intent on providing a return to their owners that they lose sight of the needs of the places where they operate. Both cities and rural areas can be hurt by this—rural areas because their physical resources are depleted and sent far away, and cities because the profit from sales to their residents goes to distant stockholders. Employment levels are controlled by decision-makers, often far removed, who do not always take into account the effects of their decisions on the local area.

What do we mean by small businesses and cooperatives?

Small businesses are firms small enough that all the employees can know each other by name. Co-ops are businesses in which the workers themselves control their work democratically. All workers have an equal voice in major decisions affecting their jobs. They also acquire equal ownership shares in the company and are its only owners.

What benefits can cities reap from small businesses and cooperatives?

- *Reinvestment in the community.* These companies are locally owned and operated, so most profits and wages are spent or reinvested in that local city or region. The money keeps circulating in the area, generating more business in town through a "multiplier effect."

- *Attention to the local impact of business decisions.* Because small businesses and co-ops are locally based and the people who make policy live in the area, they are more likely than other firms to consider the possible adverse impact of their business decisions on the community. If owners live by San Francisco Bay, they're less likely to allow their plants to pollute it than if the live in New York.

- *Local control over business.* A locally owned co-op is not going to move its operations to Taiwan simply to  improve its rate of return on investment, because if it did, the owner-workers would lose their jobs. Local control offers a sound grounding for the economy of the city.

What can cities do to promote socially responsible small businesses and cooperatives?

Here are a few proposals for municipal action that could be implemented immediately:

- Provide credit to assist people in starting or expanding locally owned businesses.

- Create "small business incubators"—places where new businesses can set up shop, pay low rent, and share services and office equipment such as computers and photocopiers with other start-ups.

- Establish zoning policies that favor neighborhood retailers as opposed to large shopping centers; permit and facilitate home businesses; and encourage mixed-use districts.

- Create easy-to-form neighborhood retail taxing districts with local boards of directors. These boards could offer mandatory commercial rent mediation and arbitration; provide rent subsidies where necessary as incentives for imaginative retail experiments; or favor foot traffic by taxing blank wall space.

- Improve local legal systems significantly (good businesses are hurt by the proximity of bad businesses). Some approaches are to create and actively support an effective District Attorney's Consumer Fraud section, to raise the amount of money below which cases are accepted by small claims courts and provide free mediation services, and to enact local laws against consumer fraud and deceptive advertising.

- Provide genuine and effective local access to cable communication services for local businesses.

- Make significant improvements in public transportation, public libraries, and low-income housing. Such a move would benefit operators of socially responsible small business.

- Develop directories of existing local businesses, benefitting both business people and people who may wish to patronize them.

Longer-term visions for municipal action

Repeal local tax codes that complicate barter and work-exchange systems.

Related fields

Most of the visions described in other sections—Renewable Energy, Urban Planting, Wild Habitat, smart Transportation, Recycling and Reuse and Celebrating Life-Place Vitality—can be implemented by existing or new local businesses.

A fable

There came a time when Jackie Franklin and her buddies

were tired of working in the Safeway produce department. Nothing personal, you understand—it was just time to strike out on their own. They liked the business and they knew a lot about vegetables, so they decided to stay in the field, but to find themselves a different market niche. After talking about it over beers after work a few times, they settled on an idea: they would pair up growers with buyers and take a small margin on the transaction. They would become, in effect, produce brokers, aiming to provide the freshest, tastiest, most nutritious fruits and vegetables to restaurants and caterers.

Jackie and her friends took this idea to the city's Office of Local Enterprise. They were pretty excited about their idea and had been in produce for a while, so the counselor thought they were a good risk. The counselor's first move was to find them an office to rent in a small business "incubator" at Mariposa and Third Streets, where they were able to share a bookkeeper, photocopier and office computer with a few other organizations while they built up their business. With a loan they obtained on the basis of their experience and business plan, they were able to lease a truck, with which they started to make runs to the organic farms in the agricultural greenbelt. Soon they were making two runs a day and could justify a second truck. By working with the bookkeeper, Jackie has learned to keep good financial records; after six months in business, her team has come to two conclusions: they're doing remarkably well, and they should probably move out of the incubator into the real world and give the benefit of the cheap space and good company to someone who needs it.

Socially responsible small businesses and cooperatives in Green City: what's possible?

In Green City, you won't find a lot of people eating mass-produced bread any more. Since the city started giving some of the same advantages to small businesses that had previously been the preserve of large corporations, small businesses of all sorts are flourishing—including neighborhood bakeries, where you can buy a loaf of warm, crusty bread that hasn't been laced with preservatives. The same thing has happened with a lot of goods that used to be available cheaper through the bigger stores and manufacturers: cheese, tofu and bookshelves now come mostly from small workshops. Small-time merchants and artisans are doing better than any time since the 1920s. People seem to prefer it this way—they want to know the person who baked their bread, to get it still warm from the oven and to be able to suggest variations in the recipe and see it on the shelf the next week. Daily life is almost like grandma had it, but better because people are conscious of having regained a sense of community that had almost slipped away.

Conclusion

The proposals in the Green City Program will create a Bay Area fundamentally different from the one in which we live now. But consider the changes brought by the invention of the automobile, television or the silicon computer chip, all of which we learned to live with. The changes in perception promoted by the Green City Program, leading to urban areas existing harmoniously with natural systems, is at least as exciting as these. Singleproposals in the Green City Program are modest in impact, but it will be the cumulative effect that counts. Each step will be small, but will lead in the direction of re-alignment toward a society that sees its long-term interest in the well-being of the whole planet.

While the Green City Program can serve as a blueprint for a more ecologically sound future, it will just remain a set of good ideas until individuals turn their energies toward implementing its goals—until people take it as their own agenda and set to work on personal, community and governmental levels to see that it gets done.

What can you do to get started? You can invest time, money and leadership in areas such as those addressed in the Green City Program with Bay Area groups already formed to work on parts of the problem. The last section of this book presents a small sample of the hundreds of ways in which volunteers can organize to "green" the future. You can encourage your local government to help transform your town into a Green City,, or if you're already in government, cut through red tape and old ideas to move it through your department.

Most importantly, you can restructure your own life to further Green City goals by recycling, by finding alternatives to the use of a private car, by buying locally grown organic produce, by revising your own energy use, and by working with others to enhance the livability of your neighborhood for both people and native plants and animals. Enormous changes in a society can come from a handful of citizen planners who restructure how they live and actively influence others.

We <u>can</u> build a society of Green Cities, where people live in harmony wih the rest of the natural world.

Opportunities for Action

There are many groups in the Bay Area that work to further the goals outlined in the Green City Program. Here are a few of the opportunities that exist for volunteers to get involved and work toward a "green" future. Please contact them directly for more details.

ABALONE ALLIANCE   (415) 861-0592
2940 Sixteenth Street   or
San Francisco, CA 94103   (415) 861-2510

Volunteer Opportunities: Research, energy analysis, newsletter printing, general office work, typesetting, layout, editing, legal and paralegal work.

AMERICAN FARMLAND TRUST   (415) 543-2098
Western Regional Office
512 Second Street
San Francisco, CA 94107

Volunteer Opportunities: Education and technical assistance to farmers, legislators and the public concerning soil, water and air quality as related to the preservation and conservation of agriculture.

AUDUBON SOCIETY   (415) 843-2222
Golden Gate Chapter
1550 Shattuck, #204
Berkeley, CA 94709

Volunteer Opportunities: Monthly conservation committee, office work, educational programming.

AUDUBON SOCIETY   (415) 388-2524
Richardson Bay Chapter
376 Greenwood Cove Road
Tiburon, CA 94920

Volunteer Opportunities: Work in naturalist bookstore, Victorian house tour guides, trail work, newsletter, special projects, community service (students), non-paying student internships (housing provided).

BAY AREA SCIENCE ASSOCIATES   (415) 383-8099
Post Office Box 431
San Francisco, CA 94101

Volunteer Opportunities: Summer only, environmental educational projects.

BUENA VISTA NEIGHBORHOOD   (415) 863-0575
ASSOCIATION
67 Divisadero Street
San Francisco, CA 94117
Volunteer Opportunities: Park reforestation.

CALIFORNIA ACADEMY OF SCIENCES   (415) 221-5100
Golden Gate Park
San Francisco, CA 94118

Volunteer Opportunities (partial listing): Research, clerical and curatorial work, outreach, exhibits, operations, education. Extensive volunteer program.

CALIFORNIA MARINE MAMMAL CENTER   (415) 331-7325
Marin Headlands
Fort Cronkhite, CA 94965

Volunteer Opportunities: Feeding/observing/direct care of animals, rescue & release, maintenance of center, sample collecting, charting, bookstore work, administration opportunities.

CALIFORNIA TROUT   (415) 392-8887
870 Market Street, #859
San Francisco, CA 94102

Volunteer Opportunities: Board of governors, various projects involving habitat restoration and enhancement for wild trout and steelhead.

CALIFORNIA NATIVE PLANT SOCIETY   (415) 435-1837
Marin Chapter
49 Seafirth Place
Tiburon, CA 94920

Volunteer Opportunities: Conservation and restoration of habitat of
native plant communities, field trips, study groups, other activities to
benefit native flora.

CALIFORNIA NATIVE PLANT SOCIETY   (415) 236-7064
San Francisco Bay Chapter
1711 Arlington Boulevard
El Cerrito, CA 94530

Volunteer Opportunities: Conservation and restoration of habitat of
native plant communities, field trips, study groups, other activities to
benefit native flora.

CALIFORNIA NATIVE PLANT SOCIETY   (415) 731-7318
Yerba Buena Chapter
309 1/2 Judah Street
San Francisco, CA 94122

Volunteer Opportunities: Conservation and restoration of habitat of
native plant communities, field trips, study groups, other activities to
benefit native flora.

COMMUNITY MEMORY PROJECT   (415) 841-1114
2617 San Pablo Avenue
Berkeley, CA 94702

Volunteer Opportunities: Community outreach, teaching, instruc-
tional work, computer work including data entry and programming.

COW HOLLOW ASSOCIATION   (415) 954-4400
345 California Street
San Francisco, CA 94104

Volunteer Opportunities: Community organizing, study of local
issues.

DESIGN ASSOCIATES WORKING   (415) 644-1315
WITH NATURE
1442 A Walnut Street
Box 101
Berkeley, CA 94709

Volunteer Opportunities: Native plant nursery propagation, restoration projects, landscaping and seed collection.

EARTH ISLAND INSTITUTE   (415) 788-3666
300 Broadway, #28
San Francisco, CA 94133

Volunteer Opportunities (partial listing): Ongoing research projects, office, clerical and outreach work; conferences & fairs, computers.

EAST BAY BICYCLE COALITION   (415) 452-1221
Post Office Box 1637
Oakland, CA 94604

Volunteer Opportunities: Office work, phone follow-ups, newsletter production, bicycle activists group.

THE ECOLOGY CENTER   (415) 548-2220
1403 Addison
Berkeley, CA 94702

Volunteer Opportunities: Many self-directed administrative, editorial, library and organizing projects.

ENVIRONMENTAL DESIGN FOUNDATION   (415) 982-2151
988 Mission Street
San Francisco, CA 94103

Volunteer Opportunities: Uses the voluntary services of architects, landscape architects and planners to assist in the preservation and improvement of the Bay Area metropolitan environment.

ENVIRONMENTAL VOLUNTEERS   (415) 424-8035
2448 Watson Court
Palo Alto, CA 94303

Volunteer Opportunities: Docents to teach natural science to children; four-month training program provided.

FORT MASON RECYCLING   (415) 285-0669
Fort Mason
San Francisco, CA 94123

Volunteer Opportunities: Seven centers. Unloading materials, office work, recordkeeping, assisting elderly and handicapped at sites. Open seven days a week.

FRIENDS OF THE RIVER   (415) 771-0400
Building C, Fort Mason
San Francisco, CA 94123

Volunteer Opportunities: Work on projects like Spring auction and conference, accounting, office work.

FRIENDS OF THE URBAN FOREST   (415) 543-5000
512 Second Street
San Francisco, CA 94107

Volunteer Opportunities: Weekly tree plantings, outreach program to make presentations to neighborhood organizations, staff educational projects at community fairs, office work and newsletter production, docents to lead tree and walking tours.

GREENBELT ALLIANCE   (415) 543-4291
116 New Montgomery, Suite 640
San Francisco, CA 94105

Volunteer Opportunities: Outreach, fundraising, administrative and office support, data entry, research, land-use planning, preservation, organizing, speaking, support work, fundraising, activism, volunteer coordination.

GREENPEACE   (415) 474-6767
Building E, Fort Mason
San Francisco, CA 94123

Volunteer Opportunities: Office work.

HAIGHT-ASHBURY SWITCHBOARD   (415) 621-6211
1338 Haight Street
San Francisco, CA 94103

Volunteer Opportunities: Phone work, update files, data transfer to computer system, fundraising. Also looking for Spanish and Asian language translators for their English publications.

H. A. N. C. RECYCLING CENTER   (415) 753-0932
780 Frederick Street
San Francisco, CA 94117

Volunteer Opportunities: Helping the public unload and sort recyclables, crushing glass and cans, general help around the yard.

HAYWARD AREA PLANNING   (415) 538-3692
ASSOCIATION
2787 Hillcrest Avenue
Hayward, CA 94542

Volunteer Opportunities: Public education and outreach, research, lobbying. (Deals with effects on Hayward area of Foothill Freeway and Walpert Ridge Development .)

INNER SUNSET COMMUNITY   (415) 644-5363
FOOD STORE
1514 Irving Street
San Francisco, CA 94122

Volunteer Opportunities: Stocking, cashiering, running the store, work on newsletter, educational materials, graphics and building. Volunteer discounts.

MISSION CREEK CONSERVANCY   (415) 585-5304
300 Channel Street, #21
San Francisco, CA 94107

Volunteer Opportunities: Wildlife inventories, public education and outreach, photography. (Mission Creek is south of Market in San Francisco.)

NEIGHBORHOOD SYSTEMS ASSOCIATION (415) 538-3692
2787 Hillcrest Avenue
Hayward, CA 94542

Volunteer Opportunities: Research projects. (Analyzes and compares densities of suburban and urban regions, especially with respect to transportation.)

THE OCEANIC SOCIETY   (415) 441-5970
Building E, Fort Mason
San Francisco, CA 94123

Volunteer Opportunities: Officework, special events, conservation task force, fact-finding group, on-site projects, training, volunteer crew members, skippers, research, educational assistants.

PEOPLE FOR A GOLDEN GATE   (415) 752-2777
NATIONAL RECREATION AREA
3627 Clement Street
San Francisco, CA 94121

Volunteer Opportunities: Lobbying, issues analysis—legal background helpful.

PLANET DRUM FOUNDATION   (415) 285-6556
Post Office Box 31251
San Francisco, CA 94131
Shasta Bioregion

Volunteer Opportunities (partial listing): Office work, research, project development, events planning publication production, Green City action.

A Green City Program

RAINFOREST ACTION NETWORK   (415) 398-4404
300 Broadway, #28
San Francisco, CA 94133
Volunteer Opportunities: Various office positions with campaign mailings, phone answering, sending orders. Also volunteer interns who assist coordinator and do research.

SAN FRANCISCO GREENS   (415) 564-8916
777 Valencia Street
San Francisco, CA 94110
Volunteer Opportunities (partial listing): Outreach, tabling, organizing, administration, library staff, advertisers, phone work, researchers, photographers, talk coordinators, letter writers, paper distribution, newsletter writing, design and production, monthly Green Calendar.

SAN FRANCISCO LEAGUE OF URBAN   (415) 468-0110
GARDENERS
2540 Newhall Street
San Francisco, CA 94124
Volunteer Opportunities: Newsletter, quarterly mailing party, office work, volunteer coordinators, library work, digging.

SAN FRANCISCO NATURAL HISTORY
Contact: Ruth Gravanis   (415) 585-5304
             Alexander Gaugine   (415) 665-3992
             Rich Hayes   (415) 776-2211

Volunteer Opportunities: Organize, lead, and attend lectures and hikes describing the land, flora and fauna of San Francisco. An all-volunteer organization.

SAN FRANCISCO TOMORROW   (415) 566-7050
942 Market Street, #505
San Francisco, CA 94102

Volunteer Opportunities: Committee positions addressing transportation, parks, open space, waterfront, large-scale development, writing of position papers, lobbying, contact with other organizations. (SFT is an urban conservation organization.)

SHARED LIVING RESOURCE CENTER   (415) 548-6608
2375 Shattuck Avenue
Berkeley, CA 94704

Volunteer Opportunities: Outreach, publications, graphics and design for organizing and developing shared living communities.

SIERRA CLUB   (415) 653-6127
Bay Chapter
6014 College Avenue
Oakland, CA 94618

Volunteer Opportunities (partial listing): Hiking trips, study groups, conservation activities, lobbying, public education and outreach..

SIERRA CLUB   (415) 552-7618
San Francisco Group

Volunteer Opportunities (partial listing): Issue study groups, commission monitoring, event planning, lobbying, city wildlife hikes.

SILICON VALLEY TOXICS COALITION   (408) 287-6707
760 North First Street
San Jose, CA 95112

Volunteer Opportunities: Outreach, various office tasks, research/ technical assistance, newsletter production, fundraising.

SPUR   (415) 781-8726
312 Sutter Street
San Francisco, CA 94108

Volunteer Opportunities: Serve on committees and write reports. (Citizen's watchdog organization focusing on social policy analysis and good government.)

THRESHOLD INTERNATIONAL CENTER   (415) 777-5299
FOR ENVIRONMENTAL RENEWAL
201 Spear Street, #1600
San Francisco, CA 94105

Volunteer Opportunities: West-coast office offers the gamut from field analysis and direct organizing to both sophisticated and apprentice office tasks.

TRAIL CENTER   (415) 968-7065
4898 El Camino Real, Office 205A
Los Altos, CA 94023

Volunteer Opportunities: Building and restoration of trails in the Bay Area. Complete training provided. Also office and committee work available.

TRI-CITY ECOLOGY CENTER   (415) 793-6222
Post Office Box 674
Fremont, CA 94537

Volunteer Opportunities: Work at recycling center, monitor wetlands and support preservation (e.g., letters, speakers, etc.), work at Household Toxics Disposal Day, support Tri-City hill preservation.

UNIVERSITY OF CALIFORNIA, BERKELEY   (415) 642-3343
BOTANICAL GARDEN
Centennial Drive
Berkeley, CA 94720

Volunteer Opportunities: Docent training, lead tours, learn propagating techniques especially for California natives.

A Green City Program
For San Francisco Bay Area Cities And Towns

Designed by Robert MacKimmie,
Beryl Magilavy and Holbrook Teter
Composed by Water Street Graphics
in Goudy Old Style
utilizing Aldus Pagemaker software
on an Apple Macintosh computer
Printed and bound by Chubasco Press
on pewter, 100%-recycled Bellbrook Laid Text
from Conservatree Paper Company